REALITIES IN AGREEMENT

POCKET EDITION

Published from
Mardukite Borsippa HQ, San Luis Valley, Colorado
Mardukite Academy & Systemology Society
for spiritual or educational purposes only

REALITIES IN AGREEMENT

SPIRITUAL LIFE AND THE UNIVERSE

A Basic Course developed
by Joshua Free
for the Systemology Society

© 2023, JOSHUA FREE

ISBN : 978-1-961509-19-1

Also available in hardcover as
"Fundamentals of Systemology"

Pocket Paperback Edition — *October 2023*

mardukite.com

SYSTEMOLOGY is the
"New Thought" of the 21st Century.

It is the study of how
Spiritual Beings with unlimited power
became entrapped in the
Human Condition.

This study is an applied philosophy
— "A Pathway to Ascension" —
that charts our way back out,
freeing the True Self to experience
higher levels of existence again.

Systemology is the true science of the
"Matrix."

After more than a decade of
development, the "Fundamentals of
Systemology" are concisely explored
here in the first official
"Basic Course" on the subject ever
given by Joshua Free for the
Mardukite Academy.

It's time to discover
who you really are...
because you
were never "Human."

Fundamentals of Systemology
Basic Course Lesson Booklets

TABLET OF CONTENTS

INTRODUCTION
TO THE
"BASIC COURSE"

WELCOME, SEEKER!
YOUR JOURNEY ON THE PATHWAY
BEGINS HERE

This is a basic course in *Systemology*—specifically, the fundamental principles of *Mardukite Systemology.*

Quite simply: *Mardukite Systemology* is a new evolution in Human understanding about the "systems" governing *Spiritual Life, Reality,* the *Universe* and all *Existences.*

In many ways, *Systemology* is a 21st Century breakthrough that continues the legacy—and unifies the original pursuits—of early 20th Century *"American New Thought"* and other metaphysical schools of philosophy and mysticism. These are mostly all generalized (and often dismissed) in modern culture as *"New Age"* beliefs, though they are actually quite "*old*"—some even based on the most ancient known writings of discovered civilizations.

Mardukite Systemology was once concisely described as "an applied spiritual technology of the 21st Century A.D., based on spiritual wisdom from the 21st Century B.C." because of our use of "*Mesopotamian*" *Arcane Tablets* as source material for its foundations (and from which it retains a "*Mardukite*" designation).

The original *New Thought Movement* in America applied a "Western Civilization" approach to "Eastern" concepts—concepts that we now take for granted today, but of which were relatively unknown to the general population at that time. The movement sought to develop an "applied spiritual philosophy" whereby an individual could unlock their hidden potentials, untapped "*Knowingness*" and higher spiritual states of *Beingness*. These innate or native conditions of *Self* (as a *Spirit*) are blocked—or "fragmented"—by a "human" preoccupation with identifying *Self* as one and the same with the material body that it is merely using as a "vehicle" to experience (communicate and interact) within *this* Physical Universe.

Early *New Thought* work primarily emphasized practical "healing" applications (*mental healing, faith healing, &tc.*)—but at its very core, we may restate the ultimate pursuit or original focus was to "free humans *to be* their ideal native spiritual state."

This goal has been with us—lingering on the periphery of the "surface world"—for much longer than the existence of a *New Thought Movement*. In fact, for as long as "spiritual beings" have found themselves entrapped by a "Human Condition" and enforced to experience *this* "material existence" (fragmented from their true *Self*), a continuing pursuit has ensued to correct the situation—at least by those individuals still retaining enough *Awareness* to realize it.

Humans have been figuring on how to break free from the *"Matrix"* for a very long time. The desire or ambition to rise above the "standard-issue" Human Condition is already there. But the truth is that many other remotely similar "evolutions" of *New Thought* have dissolved into "multi-level marketing" schemes, "motivational pop-psychology" coaching, abusive "cult-like" movements—or heavily promoted books that skyrocket to the peaks of literary "bestseller lists" only to be discarded soon after and forgotten. They all share one thing in common: they all seem to capitalize on an innate desire or yearning we have to *"ascend"*—but, of course, without delivering stable results.

Even the most pious and well-meaning

philosophies and spiritual sciences have each fallen short of piercing the *"invisible barriers"* of perception separating *this* "Physical Universe" from any other "higher" existence—and with it, blocking our "way out" and the *Awareness* of our own true native state as an *Eternal Spirit.*

SYSTEMOLOGY:
21ST CENTURY NEW THOUGHT

Our *Systemology* is a new approach to *"Self-Actualization"*—completely relevant for the modern age and the future—and quite different from previous attempts or other traditions you might find.

Former attempts at overcoming *"barriers"* or *"gates"* of *reality* have included simply pretending that they don't exist, rejecting all material existence—all *time* and *space* —as an *"illusion"* and consequently losing the ability to actually *confront* the *reality* of anything *"As-It-Is."*

Our *Systemology* is also the answer to the "great mysteries" pervading the material sciences and natural philosophies; for they only seek to further qualify and validate the *reality agreements* made for *this* Physical Universe—and thus their level of understanding can never successfully pass the "barriers" either.

When applying our philosophy and techniques, the "systematic routes" outlined for an individual to increase their *"Actualized Awareness"* (and reach gradually higher toward their *"Spiritual Ascension"*) is referred to as *"The Pathway"*—and we call that individual a *"Seeker."*

At the start of *The Pathway*, early *routes* emphasize establishing a strong personal foundation of emotional well-being and mental strength before a *Seeker* is introduced to more advanced exercises and practices.

As a *Seeker* increases their *Awareness* in this lifetime, their spiritual "*Knowingness*" also increases—which is to say their sense of "*certainty*"; a certainty on *Life*, on this and other *Universes*, but more accurately, an increased certainty on *Self* as a practically unlimited "spiritual being" *having* an enforced restrictive "human experience."

One of the goals of "*Systematic Processing*" techniques in *Systemology* is to increase the ability of a *Seeker* to actually control and direct the "*attention*" of *Self* as a "spiritual being"—and as a result, *knowingly* increase command of the "human experience." This is a part of what we mean by "*Actualized Awareness*."

THREE STATES OF KNOWINGNESS

Raising a *Seeker's* level of *Actualized Awareness* requires, by definition, "bringing what is *hidden* (or not consciously known) up into the realm of *light* or *Knowingness*." We might go as far to say, as an imperfect example, that there are three primary states of *Knowingness*: *actual knowing*, *almost knowing* and *not-knowing*.

Actual knowing is what an individual is conscious of and can easily recall as needed. It makes up our "surface" (or "above-the-surface") thoughts; what is "*actually known*" and available to *Self* for "inspection" or analytical thought. This includes what we have *certainty* on as part of our *reality*.

Then, there are other *things* "below-the-

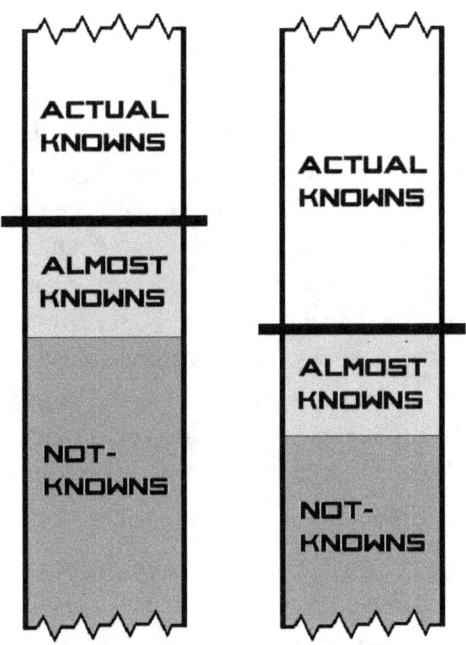

surface" that we do not easily remember (or have any *reality* on)—and these fit our other categories of *almost knowing* and *not-knowing*. The difference between these other two states is how *far* "below-the-surface" a *thing* is.

What you *"almost know"* are those *things* just "below-the-surface"—so *close* to the "surface" that they are almost accessible. This "gray area" includes what an individual is *uncertain* of. With a little assistance (*"Systematic Processing"* techniques), you can actually move a *thing* that is *"almost known"* to an "above-the-surface" state of *"actually knowing"* or remembering again. Only then may it be treated with any *certainty.*

There are also memories very deeply buried "below-the-surface." This includes suppressed data that is not currently accessible—and therefore, presently *"not-known."* Once again, there is a way to move *things* from this state into another state. For this to happen, the previous "*almost known*" *things* ("just-below-the-surface") need to be "purged" (at least partially) by "*resurfacing*" them into "*actually known*" *things*.

As more layers of "*almost knowns*" are *resurfaced* into "*actual knowns,*" more of what is "*not-known*" becomes accessible within the "gray area." *Systematic Processing* techniques of *Systemology* are intended to target this "gray area" — promoting increased *realizations* by elevating more knowledge to a state of *Actual Awareness.*

HOW TO STUDY
A SYSTEMOLOGY COURSE

Most *Seekers* study and practice *Systemology* at-a-distance and independent of the

"Mardukite Academy" or any "Master-level" mentors trained therein. This means that the *books* (and to a lesser degree, the *internet*) are the only means of direct contact a *Seeker* maintains with the "Systemology Society" during their studies.

It is quite common to have had negative past experiences with "education" and "learning"—whether in school or other type of instruction. This can sometimes inhibit an individual from pursuing a new *study* later on in their lifetime. However, simply following a few guidelines, ensures a *Seeker's* successful and positive experience when studying this course book—and, of course, the subject of *Systemology* as a whole.

To effectively study and understand a new subject (or a higher gradient of a subject), an individual must be "interested" in the material. A *Seeker* chooses to study *Systemology* because they "want" to, which is to say, on their own "*Self-Determinism.*" While modern society likes to enforce "agreement" (to further solidify a *reality*), a genuine "interest" and true "understanding" can only occur on one's own *Self-Determinism.*

Having established interest, the next *barrier* to understanding is "vocabulary" (words) and "semantics" (meaning). Any specific study, science or tradition is distinguished by the *words* used to communicate it. For true communication to occur, the intended "meaning" for each "word" used must be clearly defined and perfectly understood by the reader or receiver. We call this "*A-for-A*" or "*one-to-one*" communication.

Misunderstood words are the most common reason an individual abandons studying a subject. To relay a proper communication of *Systemology* concepts to a *Seeker*, we use very specific language in our course books. There are newer concepts that more obviously require defining when introduced; and some of our terminology uses familiar words, but with a different or specific meaning than when used elsewhere.

When a misunderstanding occurs, *Awareness* declines. These generally begin to "stack up" after the first occurrence and the level of interest and attention will also decline. This is how a "confusion" develops and the individual will get "bored" with the subject, feel tired, and unable to concentrate.

In extreme cases of confusion, there will be no future interest in studying or "looking at" something further. Feelings of "anger" and "sadness" may result (because one had originally *intended* on knowing something), followed by lower-level opposing "considerations" such as:

"didn't really want to know" or "it probably isn't very good anyways."

The misunderstood word that an individual passed in their study may not be immediately obvious. One solution is to return to the part of the material that was still interesting and enjoyable to read. When scanning around that area of text, there is likely to be a new word (or specific use of a familiar word) that is unclear, but was passed by unnoticed. All *Systemology* books include their own *glossary*. Using this *glossary* and a high-quality dictionary will help resolve this misunderstanding once it is located.

With "interest" and "understanding" secure, the next challenge of learning concerns making a subject *"tangible"* — which means handling it as a *"some-thing"* in the individual's personal *reality* or *Universe*.

Studying intellectual or "philosophical" subjects from a *book* requires excessive amounts of *"thought creation"* — of handling many conceptual images and ideas *"imagined"* solidly in one's "mind" in order to actually "look at" what one is studying. These also require a certain amount of present-time *attention* or *Awareness* to sustain a continual *creation*.

When an individual lacks "objective" examples (objects, graphic representations or direct experience) to examine, they may become "overwhelmed" by "mental-mass" if maintaining too many of their own *images*. This prompts feelings of being "worn out" or "weighed down" — and *considerations* that one "must take a break" or that the subject is "too difficult."

The obvious remedy is to supplement "book-learning" with objective or physical examples. Rather than simply studying or memorizing a series of "dry facts" from an "outside source" (and then returning to "ordinary" life), a student that does understand the material will take it up as their "own" *viewpoint*.

By taking the philosophies up as one's "own" *viewpoint*, the materially is effectively "owned" by the individual. They are not *looking* through a *lens* of someone else. The *"responsibility"* taken by this *ownership* means the freedom to apply information to everyday life and determine the truth of a matter for one's *Self*.

The final *barrier* to learning is the *knowledge* (or "know-*ledge*") itself—the *ledge* or *level* from which a person *knows* or *understands*. A "basic fact" could have many *levels* of potential understanding. To interpret *reality*, an individual "stands" on the *ledge-level* (or *gradient*) of *Knowingness* they have the most "certainty" on.

An effective education of any subject is

taught on a *gradient*. This is what is intended by introducing the study of something in *"grades."* Rather than treating a subject as one total mass, true learning is achieved by increasing one's understanding on a *gradual* incline upward. The *ascent* to a mountaintop is not successfully achieved in one leap, but by targeting and reaching specific checkpoints along the way.

In 2019, the *"Grades"* were established for the "Mardukite Academy" to properly indicate what level of understanding a specific book or course is intended for. The entry-point to directly study materials of the Systemology Society at the Academy is *"Grade-III."* Lower *grades* pertain to other *Mardukite* subjects treated separately from Systemology. Higher *grades* continue to explore the "theories and practices" of the Systemology Society as a complete *"Pathway to Ascension."*

This *Basic Course* consists of a series of lessons (booklets) that teach the *"Fundamentals of Systemology."* It is an appropriate entry-point for a new *Systemology* student. It is also applicable to more advanced *Seekers* wanting to increase their *certainty* of understanding at higher *grades* as well.

To study *Systemology* just like a student at the Academy: a *Seeker* reads through all instructional material in a *Basic Course* lesson (booklet) and then performs any practical exercises indicated at the end. Before continuing on to the next lesson (booklet), the material is read again and the light exercises are reapplied.

The second pass through the material is likely to result in different *"realizations"* (an increased *level of understanding*) than the first time. Exercises may seem more vivid or significant. *Seekers* should feel cheerful and confident in their *understan-*

ding of a section (or lesson) before pro-
ceeding even further on *The Pathway*.

YOUR FIRST STEPS ON THE
PATHWAY

Systemology is a "holistic" approach to
understanding the human experience. It
is not actually a singular "subject" in itself, but rather, a way to "view" the many
"subjects" of *Life* and all *Existence*. Its
"scope" is not restricted to the rigidly
fixed *considerations* of any one "subject"
exclusively. Yet, for us to properly communicate its specific intended meaning,
Systemology does require its own unique
basic vocabulary.

The "basic vocabulary" and *"Fundamentals"* of *Systemology* are studied together
early on *The Pathway*. They are consistent
for the remaining upper-*grades*. It is our
understanding of them that evolves as we
progress.

The entire structure of *Systemology* rests on foundations of earlier material and earlier researches—such as those found in the earlier *grades* of Mardukite Academy. However, in 2019, new developments made it possible for a *Seeker* to start upon *The Pathway* without first spending years navigating around the pitfalls of other avenues and earlier *grade* subjects. As an extension of the original Academy, the Systemology Society continues to map and define the upper-*grade routes* of our philosophy.

The *Fundamentals of Systemology* are explored throughout the *Basic Course*. The critical foundations of its vocabulary and concepts (from *Grade-II*) were concisely collected in 2019 as an essay—"*Mardukite Zuism: A Brief Introduction.*" It is summarized below to provide a more complete introduction to the "lessons" of the *Basic Course*. Each "lesson" will go on to examine this data in greater detail.

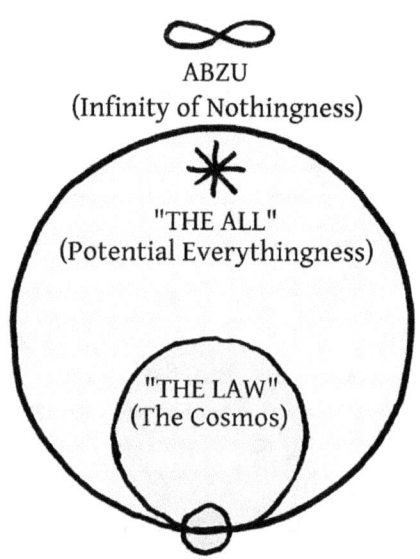

ABZU
(Infinity of Nothingness)

"THE ALL"
(Potential Everythingness)

"THE LAW"
(The Cosmos)

FOUNDATIONS OF SYSTEMOLOGY

Mardukite Zuism is a precursor to *Systemology*. It concerns an intensive archaeological study into the *Arcane Tablets* of Ancient Mesopotamia. Such tablet writings were once used to systematize an understanding of all cosmic knowledge—and they include the Babylonian *Epic of Creation*.

The *Epic of Creation* describes *ALL* ("ANKI") as separated into two *existences*: "AN" and "KI"—literally "heaven" and "earth"—which is to say *"spiritual"* ("AN") and *"physical"* ("KI"). Exterior to, and beyond, the *"potential everythingness"* of all *spiritual* existence and *physical* existence is only an Infinity of Nothingness ("ABZU").

In *Systemology*, we refer to the same two separate states of existence as *"Alpha"*

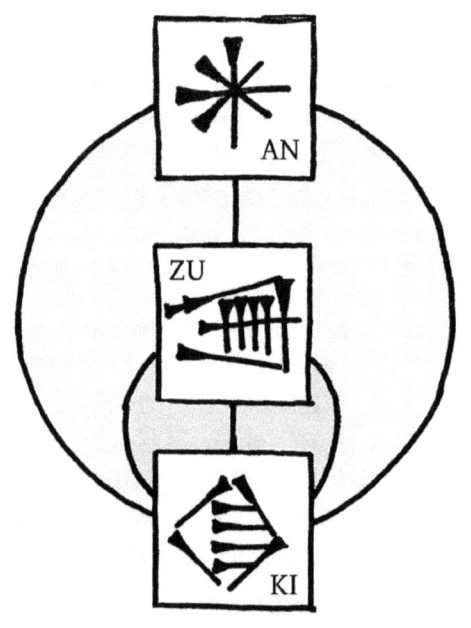

(*spiritual*) and "*Beta*" (*physical*). They are connected only by "*Spiritual Life Awareness*" or "ZU"—a term we have retained in *Systemology* (and for which *Mardukite Zuism* is named). Therefore, we have "*spiritual systems*" and "*physical systems*" connected by "ZU."

The "*Alpha*" *Universe*—of "metaphysical" or "spiritual" energy-matter—is not dependent on the "*Beta*" *Universe* to exist. The two exist independent of one another, except for a single channel or conduit maintaining a connection, which *is* the *Awareness* (the *Spiritual Life-Energy* or "ZU") of an "*Alpha-Spirit*."

"ZU" originates from an "*Alpha*" (*spiritual*) state, separate and distinct from the conditions of "*Beta*" existence that we experience as the *Physical Universe*. "ZU" is *Awareness*—the *Life-Force* or *Thought-Power* that "acts" or "impinges" on an "organism" in *Beta-Existence*.

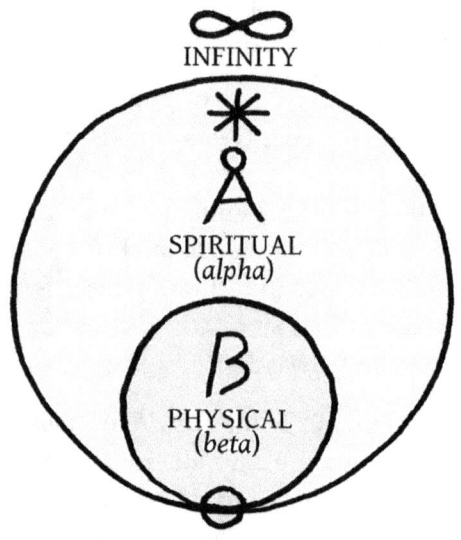

For example: the "intention" to read this book, or "commanding" a body to turn a page—those specific components are not actually a part of *this* existence. They are manifestations of a *Spiritual Awareness* (*Alpha*) acting upon an "organic body" (*Beta*). The "Alpha-Spirit" is the actual "Eternal" *Self*, which perceives and engages with *Beta-Existence* (*e.g.,* "Life on Earth") by using a "temporary" organic body or "*genetic vehicle.*"

The *Alpha-Spirit* engages a "*ZU-Line*"—a *spiritual* "life-line" of *Attention* and *Awareness* ("*ZU*") energy—to an "organic body" or *genetic-vehicle* in order to directly experience a "*physical*" *Beta-Existence.*

We use the term "*Self-Honesty*" in *Systemology* to describe the original native "*Alpha*" state of true *Self-Directed* "*Beingness*" and crystal clear "*Knowingness.*" *Self-Honesty* is the most basic "personality" or

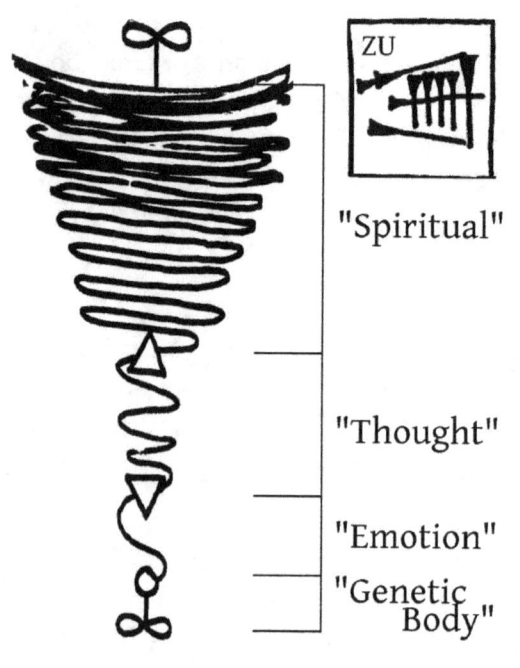

ZU

"Spiritual"

"Thought"

"Emotion"

"Genetic Body"

true expression of *Self* (*Alpha-Spirit*) as "*I-AM*"—a *Self-Determined* state that is *free* of artificial attachments, automatic reaction-response mechanisms, or enforced (*other-determined*) "*reality-agreements*" concerning the Human Condition.

Applying philosophic routes and systematic methods of *Systemology* in order to return *Awareness* of *Self* to its true "*Source*" is referred to as "*The Pathway.*" Its structure is based on archaic "models" from the "Ancient Near East" (*Mesopotamia, &tc.*) and elsewhere—such as the "*Chakras,*" the Babylonian "*Ladder of Lights*" (*Star-Gates*), and several versions of "*Kabbalah.*"

For example: the Mesopotamians built "stepped-pyramids" as temples—called "*ziggurats*"—serving to remind us of the "ZU" bridging the *spiritual* and *physical* systems. Babylonians constructed *ziggurats* to correspond with *seven* primary "steps" or "*Gates.*"

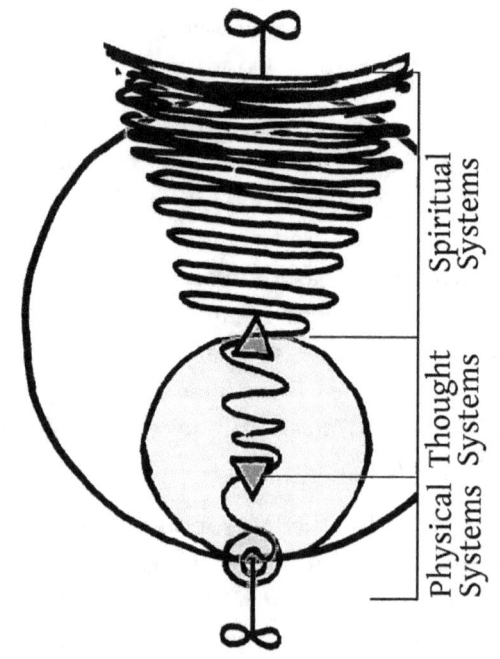

Spiritual Systems

Thought Systems

Physical Systems

The "gradients" or "tiers" of the Babylonian *Ladder of Lights* represent *The Pathway,* because they define the *levels* of *Actualized Awareness* (and *Self-Honesty*)—the states of *Self-purification*—between the "standard-issue" *Human Condition* and *Infinity.* This is the *route* we travel for our *"spiritual defragmentation"* or *Ascension.*

BASIC VOCABULARY REVIEW PUZZLE

ACROSS

3. The standard-issue default manner of filtering perceptions of the Universe, as Self is experiencing it. (*2 words*)

4. The condition of being misaligned, broken apart, shattered, fractured, distorted, or otherwise separated into parts, compared to its original state.

7. A student or practitioner studying and applying Systemology philosophy.

8. The True Self or I-AM Awareness. (2 *words, hyphenated*)

10. The nature of the Physical Universe or material existence.

11. Another way to say "the agreement about what something is."

DOWN

1. The physical body, or any organic life, may serve as your ___. (2 *words*)

2. Regimen or routine of Systemology practices, techniques or exercises that increase Actualized Awareness of Self.

5. Returning to the original native state (or Source of the Spiritual Self) is known universally as ____.

6. A stream of energy connecting Spiritual Awareness to physical existence. (2 *words, hyphenated*)

9. The progressive journey taken in Systemology is referred to as "*The* ___."

LESSON TWO:
SPIRITUAL LIFE AND
THE UNIVERSE

LESSON TWO
SPIRITUAL LIFE AND THE UNIVERSE

Our previous lesson (booklet) introduced the nature of the *Alpha-Spirit* and the basic parts involved with experiencing the standard-issue *Human Condition*. In this lesson, our focus shifts from the subjective "view" of *Self*, onto the objective environment that *Self* is "viewing"—and the *"reality"* that is being *agreed* upon.

"Spiritual techniques" of *Systemology* apply the philosophy of our *Standard Model* —which is based on the *"Arcane Tablets"* that were lost to us for thousands of years. These archaic teachings form the background of the modernized graphic depiction (and philosophy) of the *Standard Model* that we use to research practices.

The most ancient writings of cosmic wisdom essentially state: "The ALL is composed of the '*Alpha*' Spiritual Existences and the '*Beta*' Physical Existences, which are divided (or separated) by '*Cosmic Law*' and connected by a '*Spiritual Life-Awareness*' ('*ZU-Line*')—beyond which can only be an Infinity of Nothingness."

Many *Seekers* have some innate sense that while there *is* a Universe—a "world"—around us that we can *see*, this is not the "whole" of existence that we are experiencing. And by this, we do not mean other "locations" *interior* to this *Beta-Existence*. However, we can only experience what we can perceive—and those relatively higher "Gates of Perception" seem veiled to us while we are still struggling to handle the *Human Condition*.

As stated in the previous lesson: the *Alpha-Spirit* no longer practices directly handling "energy" while tied to *consider-*

ations and *reality-agreements* of *Beta-Existence*. This includes handling energies *inside* this Universe. Sound, pressure waves, light and other particles are all "sensed" by the *genetic-vehicle*, not the *Alpha-Spirit*.

Data from external sources is communicated back to the *Alpha-Spirit* through "relays" of the Mind-System. A "*ZU-Line*" connecting an *Alpha-Spirit* to, for example, an organism in *Beta-Existence*, is also the conduit or channel for communicating information between. *Fragmented* communication leads only to *confusion*.

If *Actualized*, the *Alpha-Spirit* does have an ability to *knowingly* use a "body" (a "remote point-of-view" from itself) in order to interact with, and experience, any Universe, simply by changing *agreements* about *Reality*. However, we have to own or take responsibility for such a "choice" for us to have any power to change it.

In the case of the standard-issue *Human Condition*, there is no "surface memory" of our making *reality-agreements*—and therefore, no *knowingness* to properly change them with "high power" *Awareness*. An individual must first *spot* and *realize* the point which they *actually* made a decision in order to have any *actual* intention to *change* it. How else can we change a decision we don't understand ever having made?

The *Standard Model* is the chart of our "descent" of *Awareness* as *Spiritual Beings*. It is reflected in the lore of most mystical, spiritual, and religious, teachings—yet it is never perfectly communicated or understood. By applying *Systemology*, this chart may be used to effectively reverse directions of our spiritual evolution.

INTRODUCING
THE STANDARD MODEL

The *Standard Model* of *Systemology* provides us with a foundation to explore some of the most ancient *"axioms"* of *esoteric* philosophy on a "practical" level. Seek and you will find. To know thy own *Self* is to know the Universe. As above; so below. As within; so without. As the Universe; so the *Spirit...*

Although simple in its graphic detail, the *Standard Model* required a decade of development before the first portion of its interpretation appeared as *"The Tablets of Destiny Revelation"* and *"Crystal Clear"* in 2019. All of the techniques and applications of our philosophy are actually derived from this understanding.

Originally the *Standard Model* only consisted of background models—spheres,

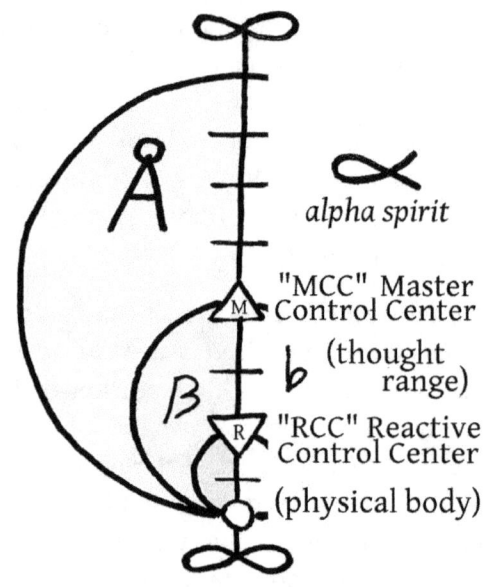

alpha spirit

"MCC" Master Control Center

(thought range)

"RCC" Reactive Control Center

(physical body)

52

circles, levels and *"Gates"*—reflected in the Mardukite (Babylonian) "Ladder of Lights," the Druid's "Cabala, and other *"cosmological" paradigms*. The *"ZU-Line"* concept developed independently. Only once we combined them did we discover an effective workable *methodology* for what was first theorized as *"Systemology: The Original Thesis"* in 2011.

On paper, it is quite basic: the *"ZU-Line"* (a spiritual or *"Alpha"* continuum of an individual's *Awareness*) intersecting various concentric circles (representing complete "systems" imposing certain conditions at different levels or gradients). Where *Awareness* "meets" environment, we have the experience of a *Reality.*

The *"ZU-Line"* is a stream of *Awareness* of the *Alpha-Spirit*—the individual as *Self*, the spiritual "I-AM." The *Alpha-Spirit* is not located in space-time, but it may operate a "point-of-view" potentially anywhere. Therefore, the *"ZU-line"* is a *"continuum"* that stretches across any and all background models of *Universes*.

Each of the circles or spheres represent a complete *"system"*—what we might even go as far to call a *"Universe."* At their own *level*, they are each a "completion" or "totality." That is not to say that they do not also in some way affect, or are affected by, other "sealed" *systems* (that only seem exclusively independent).

The study of the *Alpha-Spirit*, the *Mind*, the *genetic-vehicle*, and *Beta-Existence* can be best conducted by treating each one as a *Universe*—as a *system*. On the *Standard Model*, each circle—each *Universe*—also has its own *"continuity"* or *"zero-point."* This is also a theoretical point of communication to a "lower" system.

For *Beta-Existence*, we mean the point in which energy *"condenses"* into its most solid form of matter (or *inert matter*) for that level of existence. It may also be found at the point in which energy-matter collapses, such as with a *"black hole."* If an action takes place, it is the point where things are relatively "at rest" again.

For the *genetic-vehicle* (or *Alpha-Spirit + genetic-vehicle*), it is experienced at the point below *"apathy"* on the *"Beta-Awareness Scale"* [see *"Lesson 1"*] as "organic death." This state is reached when the *genetic-vehicle* is so overwhelmed (is the *effect*) by *Beta-Existence* that the *Alpha-Spirit* ceases to maintain its *"ZU-Line"* directly. Cellular function ceases in the biological organism, but an *Alpha-Spirit* continues its own spiritual existence.

Above "0" on our scale (or model), we have the *Spiritual Awareness* of *Life* in *Beta-Existence*. The lower levels pertain directly to the biochemical functions of the organism (*genetic-vehicle*) itself.

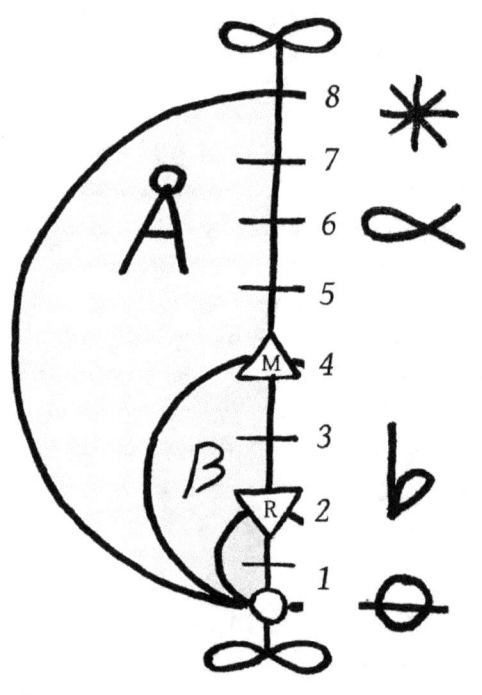

Between "0.1" and "2" we treat what is generally referred to as *"emotion"* — and *emotionally encoded* reaction-responses to data.

We consider the *emotional* range as its own *system*, because it functions like an independent Mind-System, but one that is specifically connected to *Organic Life* in *Beta-Existence*. It does not "analyze" or "reason" — but functions solely on *stimulus-response* mechanisms.

In "archaic" *Systemology*, this faculty of the *genetic-vehicle* was called the "Mind-of-Body." In today's *Standard Model*, we position the *"Reactive Control Center"* (or "RCC") at "2" on the *ZU-Line*. It governs the relay of communication between the *genetic-vehicle* and higher levels of the larger Mind-System.

Between "2.1" and "4" we treat analytical levels of attention and what is generally referred to as *"thought."* This includes portions of the Mind-System that the *Alpha-Spirit* has direct command over, so it was once referred to as the "Mind-of-Spirit"—because it is a higher faculty that is combined with the lower system.

This "archaic" interpretation is not our best understanding, because an *Alpha-Spirit* is accustomed to using the whole of the Mind-System to experience the *Human Condition*. However, we position a *"Master Control Center"* (or "MCC") at "4" on our model, indicating a point of contact between the *Alpha-Spirit* and "*Mind*."

In this wise we are able to distinguish that an *Alpha-Spirit* is operating remotely (from an *Alpha-Existence*) and *exterior* to *this* Universe (*Beta-Existence*). Through fixed attention of *Awareness*, *Self* is able to experience the *Human Condition*—and its interface or control point of a *genetic-vehicle* is the MCC of the Mind-System.

The MCC—or analytical system of *"thought"*—influences, and is influenced by, the lower-level biochemical system of *"emotion."* In turn, this system of *"emotional"* communication is what directly animates a *"body."* It is governed by the RCC, which also filters all sensory information communicated back to the *Alpha-Spirit.*

On the *Standard Model*, the boundaries of the *Human Condition*, the "Mind-System," and *Beta-Existence*, is position "4." This range of "0"-to-"4" on the *Standard-Model* is "synchronous" with the *Beta-Awareness Scale* [in *Lesson-1*]. Relatively, everything above "4" is treated as *Alpha*; that which is not tied to "being human."

In *Systemology*, a *Seeker* regains more direct command of the Mind-System (or MCC), and thereby a greater control over the related sub-systems of the Human experience. *Self-Honesty*, as it relates to *Beta-*

Existence, means having a clear *"defragmented"* channel of communication between the *"Mind"* and *genetic-vehicle.*

The position of "8" is always representative of *Infinity*—or that which is beyond what we can identify as the native original state of the *Spiritual Self* (or *Alpha-Spirit*) at "7" on our *Standard Model.* This is the level of one's own "personal" *Home Universe.* And here we see the ancient "seven-stepped pathway" to *Self.*

Technically, an individual has never actually "left" its native state; but it can *consider* that it has. Not actually being a locatable position an *Alpha-Spirit* may potentially *consider* being as *any* position. Of course, those *considerations* become more limited as one takes on more *layers* of "personality" and "character."

When fixated on the *Human Condition* and *Beta-Existence,* the *Standard Model* is able to chart the various "positions" of

Beingness that an individual is considering *Self* to *be*. The lower the level of *Beta-Awareness*, the lower the point of *Beingness* that is being determined *for* the *Alpha-Spirit*, whose own true *Beingness* and ideal state of *Awareness* is not positioned *interior* to Beta-Existence, but from an *exterior* point-of-view.

The remaining *Alpha* domain on our *Standard Model* is reserved for the subjects of *"Alpha-Thought"* —and the "creations" and "games" that an individual engaged in preceding the *Human Condition* and *Beta-Existence*. It still relates to a Human experience in terms of *"intention"* and *"imagination"* —which are *Alpha* qualities.

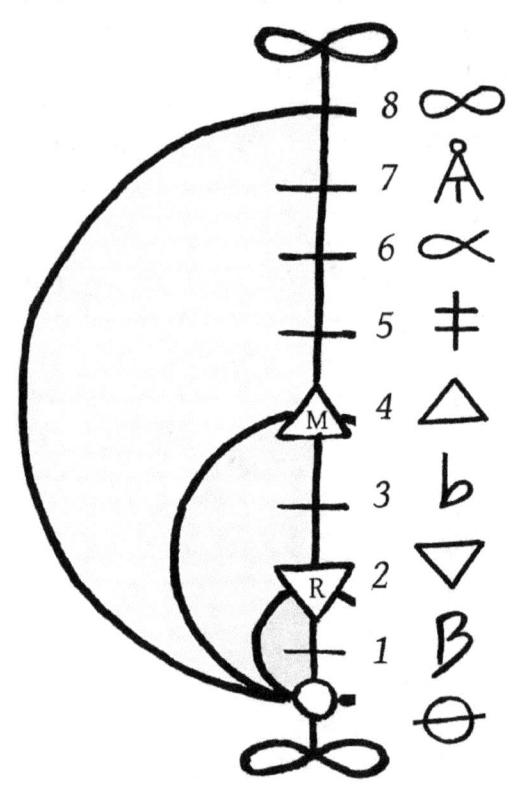

8 ∞

7 Å

6 ∝

5 ‡

4 △

3 b

2 ▽

1 B

⊖

THE STANDARD MODEL OF SYSTEMOLOGY

-- *ALPHA* --

8. "INFINITY"
7. The Alpha-Spirit (*Home Universe*)
6. Alpha-Thought (*Creation and Imagination*)
5. Will-Intention (*Alpha Equivalent of Effort*)

-- *BETA* --

4. "MCC" (*Command of a Mind*)
3. Analytical (*Associative Knowledge*)
2. "RCC" (*Control of Biochemical Activity*)
1. Emotional (*Stored Data of Loss and Pain*)
0. Effort (*Solidity of the Physical Universe*)

THE SPHERES OF BETA-EXISTENCE

The *Standard Model* takes an "objective" view of *all* potential positions of *all* potential *Universes*. It is an illustration of "spiritual descent," but also a map to chart the way back toward *Ascension*. Additional work with this model resulted in the development of an alternative "subject" view called the *Spheres of Existence*.

It has been suggested in our philosophy that the *Alpha-Spirit* departed from their own original native state in order to "create" with other *Alpha-Spirits*—or else to shift *Awareness* from a personal *"Home Universe"* to a *"Shared Universe."* The *Alpha-Spirit* is still very much operating from a "personal universe"—however, in this case, the individual *alters* it to also simultaneously "share" the *reality* of other entities by *"agreement."*

As an individual takes on more layers of *agreements*—and *fragmentation*—the qualities and considerations of a "personal universe" continue to "condense"—or "collapse"—into lower levels of *Knowingness* and *Beingness*. The apparent result of this "descending spiral" has led us to such a state as the *Human Condition*.

From the perspective of experiencing the *Human Condition* in *Beta-Existence*, the solution to our *Ascension* is to "free up" the entanglement of our *Awareness* and *considerations*; to "extend" rather than "retract" our "*spiritual reach*"; to rehabilitate the native *Self-Honest willingness* to *confront* all potential existence "*As-It-Is*."

The *Systemology* "*Spheres of Existence*" chart allows us to systematically gauge this "*spiritual reach*" from the perspective of the *Alpha-Spirit*, operating as a *genetic-vehicle* in *Beta-Existence*. *Alpha-Spirits* operate toward some "goal"—as in a "*game*." And the common denominator of "*games*" in this *Beta-Existence* is to *survive*.

Ideal activities and "goals" of the *Alpha-Spirit* are all *creative*. Hence, the most optimum level of *survival* in *Beta-Existence* is achieved by effectively applying *Alpha* qualities—*imagination, reason, ethics* and *aesthetics*—to the Human experience. Even prior to reaching *Ascension*, we can improve qualities of *Life* here on Earth.

Our "*Spheres of Existence*" philosophy only partly aligns with the *Standard Model*. It begins with "*Self*" at "1" and extends outward into "existence" from there—as does our *reach*. At "1" we identify the individual as an entity in *Beta-Existence* operating a material "Body." The individual is a singular unit of *Spiritual Awareness* (or *ZU-Line*) "impinging" on the Physical Universe.

This philosophy can apply to *any* individual "lifeform" or "consciousness" on *any* planet of *Beta-Existence*. It is simply the case that we are accustomed to viewing such metaphysical models—the Babylonian *Ladder of Lights*, the Druid's *Cabala*, the *Chakras*, *&tc.*—from the perspective of the *Human Condition* on *this* planet.

In "archaic" *Systemology*, we referred to this model as "Circles of Influence." Each circle is a "system" unto itself, and they do mostly stretch "horizontally" across *Beta-Existence*. However, they are better depicted as encompassing (or surrounding the whole) of one another as a series of "spheres" within "spheres." As they represent the nature of *this* existence and the game-goal *"to exist,"* the newer terminology is more accurate.

THE SPHERES OF EXISTENCE SYSTEMOLOGY MODEL

– – *METAHUMAN* – –

8. "INFINITY"
7. Alpha (*All Life in Spiritual Existence*)
6. Universe (*All Life in Beta-Existence*)
5. Planet (*All Life on Earth, Trees,
                                Animals...*)

– – *HUMAN* – –

4. Species (*All Humans*)
3. Societies (*Groups, Organizations*)
2. Home (*Domestic, Family, Children*)
1. Self (*The Individual*)

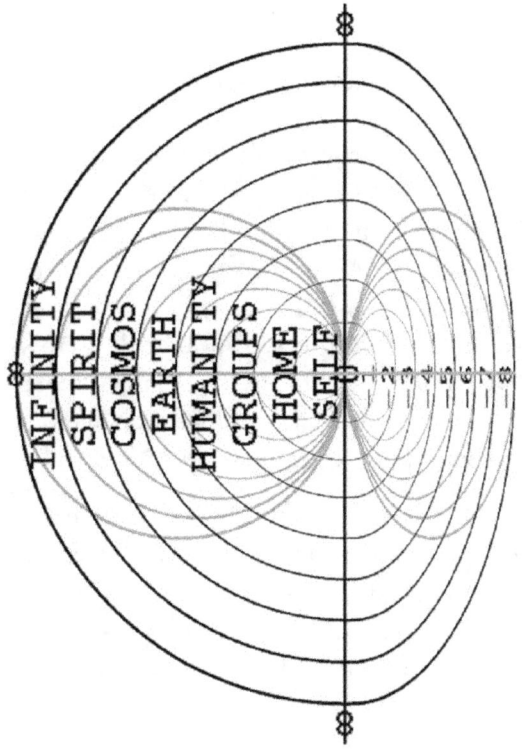

INFINITY
SPIRIT
COSMOS
EARTH
HUMANITY
GROUPS
HOME
SELF

69

REACHING THROUGH THE SPHERES

There are many goal-oriented purposes for the activities of *Spiritual Life*. However, in regards to the *Human Condition* (*Alpha-Spirit* + *genetic-vehicle*), the Primary Directive or motivation pertains to material survival. When we say *"to survive"* (or *"to exist"*) it does not simply mean barely scraping by just to see another day. However, an individual that *is* "surviving to see another day" must at least be evaluating *something* right.

The *Spheres of Existence* are *"existential."* They pertain to the experience of conditions *in* existence—domains that support, and are supported by, various systems of *Life.* Many individuals fix attention on one specific domain—yet these are all interconnected systems essentially equal to one another to support *Actualization.*

70

In many ways, *Self-Actualization* is proportional to the ability to "reach across the spheres." This is similar to how *Actualized Awareness* is equivalent to how much *defragmented* clear communication is relayed across the *ZU-Line* of the *Standard Model*. Data from these models assists in effectively applying our techniques.

Individuals are indeed themselves ("1"); they live in homes, and perhaps have a family ("2"); work jobs and participate in societal groups ("3"); and, of course, are members of the *human* species ("4"); one of many species of this ecosystem on Earth ("5"); and so on. What is not generally equal is how *Self-Honest* or *Actualized* an individual actually is in their clear understanding and communication at all of these *levels*.

Each of these *Spheres of Existence* is composed of many specific aspects or "*fa-*

cets"—some of which are likely to have more "turbulent" energy entangled up in them than others. Any such associated turbulence—or *fragmentation*—affects the clear handling of these *facets* of existence and achievement of total *Actualization*.

An individual generally develops a "personality" of inclinations or patterns based on stored experiences. The tendency to "reach toward" or "retract away" from one or another *facet* becomes automatic. While an *Alpha-Spirit* is certainly entitled to prefer one or another interest, automated tendencies are not very *godlike*.

Those that are not *Actualized* at the first sphere of "*Self*" may still continue to operate a *fragmented* reach out to other spheres by their interconnected interaction. One person may believe raising a family is the most important thing, while another neglects theirs for a career, or to save a forest. They are seldom all balanced.

The *Spheres of Existence* model also plays a significant role in upper-grade studies regarding *"Utilitarian Systemology"* — which is to say, *ethics*. In brief: the "greatest good" or "ideal course of action" is that which helps, promotes, or assists, continued "optimum survival" at the highest sphere or *Life-System* of existence.

When we reactively *"withdraw"* from some *facet* of *reality* — something we've already *agreed* is *real* — then we are not willing (and therefore "unable") to *confront* it *"As-It-Is."* These "reactive mechanisms" are a source of *fragmentation*, because they still require part of our *Awareness* (or energy) to continue beneath the surface.

The key *realization* for a *Seeker* to maintain while pursuing their *Systemology* studies is that at our core — our native state — we are *Spiritual Beings* with essentially unlimited power to *create*. The track of our spiritual existence is an accumulated series of descending considerations and *reality-agreements*.

Systematically, we must work our way out to uncover the secret of how an *Alpha-Spirit* allowed itself to be entrapped in these ongoing *games* of *survival*, when the one thing an *Eternal Being* cannot help but continue doing, *is* survive.

PRACTICE EXERCISES

1. While seated in a chair, *get the sense* of *You* "making" *that body* "sit" in a chair. [Practice this several times or until you have a *reality* on it being so; then continue reading.] Perform the same basic exercise, this time applying it to whatever the "body" is doing. For example: if you are holding this book, then *get the sense* of *You* "making" *that body* "hold" this book. The *Human Condition* is accustomed to frequently functioning on "automatic" reactive-responses. This applies not only to cycles of thought and emotion, but also the pattern of our behaviors. We are often not in a habit of

thinking, feeling, and acting, *deliberately*. Therefore, take some time each day to *knowingly* command the Human experience by practicing this exercise. At first, you may only maintain a few minutes of *conscious control* before attention drifts. Eventually, you will be able to increase the duration you can hold this concept, and extend your application of this "sense" to more and more of everyday *Life*.

2. On a blank sheet of paper, draw out your own version of the *Spheres of Existence* model. Begin with the smallest circle—labeling it "SELF"—and then proceed to draw the other seven circles around it, using the list from this lesson to label them, too. Inside the space you've provided to represent each "*Sphere*," list as many

words—aspects or *facets*—that you "associate" with that specific domain. It is most beneficial to *identify* actual "things" or "beings"—with "mass"—but feel free to include any "concepts" that also surface. If space on your model becomes too restrictive and you are having to be too general, you can continue your listing on separate sheets of paper. Some examples from other *Systemology* materials include: ("1") *Self, Your Body*; ("2") *Home, Family, A Specific Relation, Sex, Children*; ("3") *Groups, Community, A Certain Group, A Certain Type of Person*; ("4") *Human Species, Nationalities*; ("5") *Planet Earth, Animals, Nature*; ("6") *A Solar System, Galaxies, Physical Universe*; ("7") *Spirits, Entities, Mysticism*; ("8") *Infinity, God, Religion*.

3. Start a notebook to keep records of your practices as written exercises. Record any data from the exercises and any realizations that occur as a result. Using the list you prepared in the previous exercise: consider (or reflect on) what your feelings are concerning each listed item. What items do you prefer and which do you dislike? Recall individual times when you had encounters with each item. What have you done about (or toward) the item? What has that item done to you? What have you observed others do about (or act toward) the item? How has the accumulation of experiences (regarding a particular item) affected your inclinations to either like or avoid it. How does having a particular "belief" or "feeling" about an item affect

what you are now willing to experience?

4. Spend some time outdoors—or looking out through a window—and see how many forms of *Life* you can *identify* as existing in your surrounding environment. Take notice of the things you can actually *see*. In each case, consider (or reflect on) *"what" Life* is actually *doing*. Then consider what *Sphere of Existence* it best applies to. Finally, consider what relationship it has with other *Life*: How is its continued existence supporting, or being supported by, other *Spheres of Existence? Systemology* is named for its approach of studying existence as a composite of "living" or "dynamic" (variable) *systems*. Humans are accustomed to treating *reality* as both solidly fixed *and* fragmented

into a myriad of unrelated parts. By looking closely and fixedly from one "point-of-view" we exclude all others. We forget that everything we *see* is interconnected—even connected to levels of existence that we are not presently perceiving. *Self-Actualization* increases with the range of existence that an individual is *willing* to (but is not required to) extend its "*spiritual reach*" toward and experience.

5. Go to a public place where you can directly observe the activities of *Life* and directly notice various things around you. *Identify* specific examples of each of the *Spheres of Existence* in your surroundings. You may begin with the *Lifeforms* and various "things" that you first *notice*, and then assigning their place on the model.

Secondly, you may take each category (or existential system) in turn and *spot* the items in your environment that apply to that specific *Sphere of Existence.*

6. Taking individual *Spheres of Existence* in turn, *imagine* the world from the "point-of-view" of each one exclusively. Record any *realizations* that you have while performing this exercise.

7. Locate an object in your environment. *Decide* that you will *reach* for the object; then *decide* to "make" the "body" do so—and finally *do* it. Now, *decide* that you will *let-go* of the object; *intend* to "make" the "body" do so—and then *let-go*. Practice this exercise of *knowingly* locating, then "reaching to touch" and "retracting your touch," for different ob-

jects. Then, choose a large enough object that you can practice this exercise repeatedly for different *spots* on the same object. The *Human Condition* is full of "automatic mechanisms" and "reactive-responses" that seem to affect control of the "body" and place the *Alpha-Spirit* at an "effect" point, rather than "cause." Tendencies to *hold onto* or suddenly *withdraw from* various aspects, persons, or *facets* of *Life*, often take place outside of one's conscious (or *Actualized*) *Awareness*. Although we might apply "reason" or "justification" after the fact, the truth is that the *Alpha-Spirit* operates best from a "defragmented" state of *Self-Honesty*—fully *Self-Determined* in all of its creative expressions, directed attention, and intentions for action.

Continue learning
The Fundamentals of Systemology
in your next
Basic Course
lesson booklet:

WINDOWS TO EXPERIENCE:
FILTERS OF HUMAN PERCEPTION

GLOSSARY

actualization : to make actual, not just potential; to bring into full solid Reality; to realize fully in *Awareness* as a "thing."

agreement (reality) : unanimity of opinion of what is "thought" to be known; an accepted arrangement of how things are; things we consider as "real" or as an "is" of "reality"; a consensus of what is real as made by standard-issue (common) participants; what an individual contributes to or accepts as "real"; in *Systemology*, a synonym for "*reality.*"

alpha : the first, primary, basic, superior or beginning of some form; in *Systemology*, referring to the state of existence operating on spiritual archetypes and postulates, will and intention "exterior" to the low-level condensation and solidarity of energy and matter as the 'physical universe'.

alpha-spirit : a "spiritual" *Life*-form; the "true" *Self* or I-AM; the *individual*; the spiritual (*alpha*) *Self* that is animating the (*beta*) physical body or "*genetic vehicle*" using a continuous *Lifeline* of spiritual ("*ZU*") energy; an individual spiritual (*alpha*) entity possessing no physical mass or measurable waveform (motion) in the Physical Universe as itself, so it animates the (*beta*) physical body or "*genetic vehicle*" as a catalyst to experience *Self*-determined causality in effect within the *Physical Universe*; a singular unit or point of *Spiritual Awareness* that is *Aware* that it is *Aware*.

alpha thought : the highest spiritual *Self-determination* over creation and existence exercised by an Alpha-Spirit; the Alpha range of pure *Creative Ability* based on direct postulates and considerations of *Beingness*; spiritual qualities comparable to "thought" but originating in Alpha-existence (at "6.0") independently superior to a *beta-anchored* Mind-System, although an Alpha-Spirit may use Will ("5.0") to carry the intentions of a postulate or consideration ("6.0") to the Master Control Center ("4.0").

ascension : actualized *Awareness* elevated to the point of true "spiritual existence" exterior to *beta existence*. An "Ascended Master" is one who has returned to an incarnation on Earth as an inherently *Enlightened One*, demonstrable in their actions—they have the ability to *Self-direct* the "Spirit" as *Self* and maintain consciousness beyond this existence as a personal identity continuum with the same *Self-directed* control

85

and communication of Will-Intention that is exercised, actualized and developed deliberately during one's present incarnation.

associative knowledge : significance or meaning of a facet or aspect assigned to (or considered to have) a direct relationship with another facet; to connect or relate ideas or facets of existence with one another; a reactive-response image, emotion or conception that is suggested by (or directly accompanies) something other than itself; in traditional systems logic, an equivalency of significance or meaning between facets or sets that are grouped together, such as in $(a + b) + c = a + (b + c)$; in NexGen Systemology, erroneous associative knowledge is assignment of the same value to all facets or parts considered as related (even when they are not actually so), such as in $a = a, b = a, c = a$ and so forth without distinction.

attention : active use of *Awareness* toward a specific aspect or thing; the act of "attending" with the presence of *Self*; a direction of focus or concentration of *Awareness* along a particular channel or conduit or toward a particular terminal node or communication termination point; the Self-directed concentration of personal energy as a combination of observation, thought-waves and consideration; focused application of *Self-Directed Awareness*.

awareness : the highest sense of-and-as Self in knowing and being as I-AM (the *Alpha-Spirit*); the extent of beingness directed as a POV experienced by Self as knowingness.

beta (awareness) : all consciousness activity ("*Awareness*") in the "Physical Universe" (KI) or else *beta-existence*; *Awareness* within the range of the *genetic-body*, including material thoughts, emotional responses and physical motors; personal *Awareness* of physical energy and physical matter moving through physical space and experienced as "time"; the *Awareness* held by *Self* that is restricted to a physical organic *Lifeform* or "*genetic vehicle*" in which it experiences causality in the *Physical Universe*.

beta (existence) : all manifestation in the "Physical Universe" (KI); the "Physical" state of existence consisting of vibrations of physical energy and physical matter moving through physical space and experienced as "time"; the conditions of *Awareness* for the *Alpha-spirit* (*Self*) as a physical organic *Lifeform* or "*genetic vehicle*" in which it experiences causality in the *Physical Universe*.

beta-defragmentation : toward a state of *Self-Honesty* in regards to handling experience of the "Physical Universe" (*beta-existence*); an applied spiritual philosophy (or technology) of Self-Actualization

condense (condensation) : the transition of vapor to liquid; denoting a change in state to a more substantial or solid condition; leading to a more compact or solid form.

consideration : careful analytical reflection of all aspects; deliberation; determining the significance of a "thing" in relation to similarity or dissimilarity to other "things"; evaluation of facts and importance of certain facts; thorough examination of all aspects related to, or important for, making a decision; the analysis of consequences and estimation of significance when making decisions.

continuity : being a continuous whole; a complete whole or "total round of"; the balance of the equation ["–120" + "120" = "0" *&tc.*]; an apparent unbroken interconnected coherent whole; also, as applied to Universes in *Systemology*, the lowest base consideration of space-time or commonly shared level of energy-matter apparent in an existence, or else the lowest degree of solidity or condensation whereby all mass that exists is identifiable or communicable with all other mass that exists; represented as "0" on the *Standard Model* for the Physical

Universe (*beta-existence*), a level of existence that is below Human emotion, comparable to the solidity of "rocks" and "walls" and "inert bodies."

defragmentation : the *reparation* of wholeness; collecting all dispersed parts to reform an original whole; a process of removing "*fragmentation*" in data or knowledge to provide a clear understanding; applying techniques and processes that promote a *holistic* interconnected *alpha* state, favoring observational *Awareness* of continuity in all spiritual and physical systems; in *Systemology*, a "*Seeker*" achieving an actualized state of basic "*Self-Honest Awareness*" is said to have completed *beta-defragmentation*, whereas *Alpha-defragmentation* is the rehabilitation of the *creative ability*, managing the *Spiritual Timeline* and the POV of *Self* as Alpha-Spirit (I-AM).

existence : the *state* or fact of *apparent manifestation*; the resulting combination of the Principles of Manifestation: consciousness, motion and substance; continued *survival*; that which independently exists.

exterior : outside of; on the outside; in *Systemology*, we mean specifically the POV of *Self* that is '*outside of*' the *Human Condition,* free of the physical and mental trappings of the Physical

Universe; a metahuman range of consideration; see also '*Zu-Vision*'.

external : a force coming from outside; inform-ation received from outside sources; in *System-ology*, the objective *'Physical Universe'* existence, or *beta-existence*, that the Physical Body or *genetic vehicle* is essentially *anchored* to for its considerations of locational space-time as a dimension or POV.

facets : an aspect, an apparent phase; one of many faces of something; a cut surface on a gem or crystal; in *Systemology*—a single per-ception or aspect of a memory or "*Imprint*"; any one of many ways in which a memory is recor-ded; perceptions associated with a painful emo-tional (sensation) experience and "*imprinted*" onto a metaphoric lens through which to view future similar experiences; other secondary ter-minals that are associated with a particular ter-minal, painful event or experience of loss, and which may exhibit the same encoded signific-ance as the activating event.

fragmentation : breaking into parts and scatter-ing the pieces; the *fractioning* of wholeness or the *fracture* of a holistic interconnected *alpha* state, favoring observational *Awareness* of per-ceived connectivity between parts; *discontinu-ity*; separation of a totality into parts; in *System-*

ology, a person outside a state of *Self-Honesty* is said to be *fragmented*.

genetic-vehicle : a physical *Life*-form; the physical (*beta*) body that is animated/controlled by the (*Alpha*) *Spirit* using a continuous *Lifeline* (ZU); a physical (*beta*) organic receptacle and catalyst for the (*Alpha*) *Self* to operate "causes" and experience "effects" within the *Physical Universe*.

gradient : a degree of partitioned ascent or descent along some scale, elevation or incline; "higher" and "lower" values in relation to one another.

holistic : the examination of interconnected systems as encompassing something greater than the *sum* of their "parts."

imagination : the ability to create *mental imagery* in one's Personal Universe at will and change or alter it as desired; the ability to create, change and dissolve mental images on command or as an act of will; to create a mental image or have associated imagery displayed (or "conjured") in the mind that may or may not be treated as real (or memory recall) and may or may not accurately duplicate objective reality; to employ *creative abilities* of the Spirit that are independent of reality agreements with beta-existence.

intention : directed application of Will; to intend (have "in Mind") or signify (give "significance" to) for or toward a particular purpose; in *Systemology* (from the *Standard Model*)—the spiritual activity at WILL (5.0) directed by an *Alpha Spirit* (7.0); the application of WILL as "Cause" from a higher order of Alpha Thought and consideration (6.0).

interior : inside of; on the inside; in *Systemology*, we mean specifically the POV of *Self* that is fixed to the *'internal'* Human Condition, including the *Reactive Control Center* (RCC) and Mind-System or *Master Control Center* (MCC); within *beta-existence*.

internal : a force coming from inside; information received from inside sources; in *Systemology*, the objective experience of *beta-existence* associated with the Physical Body or *genetic vehicle* and its POV regarding sensation and perception; from inside the body; in the body.

Human Condition : a standard default state of Human experience, generally accepted to be the extent of its potential identity (*beingness*).

imprint : to strongly impress, stamp, mark (or outline) onto a softer 'impressible' substance; to mark with pressure onto a surface; in *Systemology*, used to indicate permanent Reality impressions marked by frequencies, energies or inter-actions experienced during periods of emotional distress, pain, unconsciousness, loss, enforce-ment, or something antagonistic to physical (personal) survival, all of which are are stored with other reactive response-mechanisms at lower-levels of *Awareness* as opposed to the act-ive memory database and proactive processing center of the Mind; an experiential "memory-set" that may later resurface—be triggered or stimulated artificially—as Reality, of which similar responses will be engaged automatic-ally; holographic-like imagery "stamped" onto consciousness as composed of energetic *facets* tied to the "snap-shot" of an experience.

knowledge : clear personal processing of in-formed understanding; information (data) that is actualized as effectively workable understand-ing; a demonstrable understanding on which we may 'set' our *Awareness*—or literally a "know-ledge."

Master-Control-Center (MCC) : a perfect computing device to the extent of the informa-tion received from "lower levels" of sensory ex-perience/perception; the proactive communicat-ion system of the "*Mind*"; a relay point of act-ive *Awareness* along the Identity's *ZU-line*, which is responsible for maintaining basic *Self-*

Honest clarity of *Knowingness* as a *seat of consciousness* between the *Alpha-Spirit* and the secondary "*Reactive Control Center*" of a *Life-form* in *beta existence*; the Mind-center for an *Alpha-Spirit* to actualize cause in the *beta existence*; the analytical *Self-Determined* Mind-center of an *Alpha-Spirit used* to project *Will* toward the genetic body; the point of contact between *Spiritual Systems* and the *beta existence*; presumably the "*Third Eye*" of a being connected directly to the *I-AM-Self*, which is responsible for *determining* Reality at any time; in *Systemology*, this is plotted at (4.0) on the continuity model of the *ZU-line*.

mental image : a subjectively experienced "picture" created and imagined into being by the Alpha-Spirit (or at lower levels, one of its automated mechanisms) that includes all perceptible *facets* of totally immersive scene, which may be forms originated by an individual, or a "facsimile-copy" ("snap-shot") of something seen or encountered; a duplication of wave-forms in one's Personal Universe as a "picture" that mirror an "external" Universe experience, such as an *Imprint*.

point-of-view (POV) : a point to view from; an opinion or attitude as expressed from a specific identity-phase; a specific standpoint or vantage-point; a definitive manner of consideration specific to an individual phase or identity; a place or position affording a specific view or vantage; circumstances and programming of an individual that is conducive to a particular response, consideration or belief-set (paradigm); a position (consideration) or place (location) that provides a specific view or perspective (subjective) on experience (of the objective). May also be referred to in our texts as a "*viewpoint.*"

processing, systematic : the inner-workings or "through-put" result of systems; in *Systemology*, a methodology of applied spiritual technology used toward personal Self-Actualization; methods of selective directed attention, communicated language and associative imagery that targets an increase in personal control of the human condition.

reactive control center (RCC) : the secondary (reactive) communication system of the "*Mind*"; a relay point of *Awareness* along the Identity's *ZU-line*, which is responsible for engaging basic motors, biochemical processes and any *programmed automated responses* of a living *beta* organism; the reactive Mind-Center of a living organism relaying communications of *Awareness* between causal experience of *Physical Systems* and the "*Master Control Center*";

it presumably stores all emotional encoded imprints as fragmentation of *ZU* (within the range of the "*psychological/ emotive systems*" of a being), which it may *react* to as Reality at any time; in *Systemology*, this is plotted at (2.0) on the continuity model of the *ZU-line*.

reality : see "*agreement.*"

Seeker : an individual on the *Pathway to Self-Honesty*; a practitioner of *Mardukite Systemology* or *Systemology Processing* that is working toward *Spiritual Ascension*.

Self-actualization : bringing the full potential of the Human spirit into Reality; expressing full capabilities and creativeness of the *Alpha-Spirit*.

Self-determinism : the freedom to act, clear of external control or influence; the personal control of Will to direct intention.

Self-honesty : the basic or original *alpha* state of *being* and *knowing*; clear and present total *Awareness* of-and-as *Self*, in its most basic and true proactive expression of itself as *Spirit* or *I-AM*—free of artificial attachments, perceptive filters and other emotionally-reactive or mentally-conditioned programming imposed on the human condition by the systematized physical world; the ability to experience existence without judgment.

Spheres of Existence (dynamic systems) : a model of *eight* concentric circles, rings or spheres (each larger than the former) that is overlaid onto the Standard Model of Beta-Existence to demonstrate dynamic systems of existence extending out from a POV of Self (often as a "body") at the *First Sphere*; these are given as a basic eightfold system: *Self, Home/Family, Groups, Humanity, Life on Earth, Physical Universe, Spiritual Universe* and *Infinity-Divinity*.

Standard Model, The (systemology) : our existential and cosmological *standard model* or cabbalistic model; a "*monistic continuity model*" demonstrating *total system* interconnectivity "above" and "below" observation of any apparent *parameters*; the original presentation of the *ZU-line*, represented as a singular vertical (*y*-axis) waveform in space across dimensional levels or Universes (*Spheres of Existence*) without charting any specific movement across a dimensional time-graph *x*-axis; The Standard Model of Systemology represents the basic workable synthesis of common denominators in models explored throughout Grade-I and Grade-II material.

system : from the Greek, "to set together"; to set or arrange things or data together so as to form an orderly understanding of a "whole."

thought-form : apparent *manifestation* or existential *realization* of *Thought-waves* as "solids" even when only apparent in Reality-agreements of the Observer; the treatment of *Thought-waves* as permanent *imprints* obscuring *Self-Honest* clarity of *Awareness* when reinforced by emotional experience as actualized "thought-formed solids" ("*beliefs*") in the Mind; energetic patterns that "surround" the individual.

ZU : the ancient Sumerian cuneiform sign for the archaic verb—"*to know*," "*knowingness*" or "*awareness*"; in *Mardukite Zuism and Systemology*, the active energy/matter of the "Spiritual Universe" (AN) experienced as a *Lifeforce* or *consciousness* that imbues living forms extant in the "Physical Universe" (KI); "*Spiritual Life Energy*"; energy demonstrated by the WILL of an actualized *Alpha-Spirit* in the "Spiritual Universe" (AN), which impinges its *Awareness* into the Physical Universe (KI), animating/controlling *Life* for its experience of *beta-existence* along an individual Alpha-Spirit's personal *Identity-continuum*, called a *ZU-line*.

Zu-Line : a theoretical construct in *Mardukite Zuism and Systemology* demonstrating *Spiritual Life Energy* (*ZU*) as a personal individual "continuum" of Awareness interacting with all Spheres of Existence on the Standard Model of

Systemology; a spectrum of potential variations and interactions of a monistic continuum or singular *Spiritual Life Energy (ZU)* demonstrated on the Standard Model; an energetic channel of potential POV and "locations" of Beingness, demonstrated in early Systemology materials as an individual Alpha-Spirit's personal *Identity-continuum*, potentially connecting *Awareness (ZU)* of *Self* with "*Infinity*" simultaneous with all points considered in existence; a symbolic demonstration of the "*Life-line*" on which *Awareness (ZU)* extends from the direction of the "Spiritual Universe" (AN) in its true original *alpha state* through an entire possible range of activity resulting in its *beta state* and control of a *genetic-entity* occupying the *Physical Universe (KI)*.

Zu-Vision : the true and basic (*Alpha*) Point-of-View (perspective, POV) maintained by *Self* as *Alpha-Spirit* outside boundaries or considerations of the *Human Condition* "Mind-Systems" and *exterior* to beta-existence reality agreements with the Physical Universe; a POV of Self *as* "a unit of Spiritual Awareness" that exists independent of a "body" and entrapment in a *Human Condition*; "spirit vision" in its truest sense.

THE SYSTEMOL

Seekers and students of the *Basic Course* and *Professional Course* will also be interested in the *Advanced Series* of the *Systemology Core*. These volumes are a complete chronological record of the Mardukite New Thought developments from the Systemology Society, published in 2019 through 2023.

The *Systemology Core* begins with the first professional publication released when the *Mardukite Systemology Society* emerged from the underground in 2019, with: *"The Tablets of Destiny Revelation."*

OGY PATHWAY

The Tablets of Destiny Revelation:
*How Long-Lost Anunnaki Wisdom
Can Change the Fate of Humanity*

Crystal Clear: *Handbook for Seekers*

Metahuman Destinations (*2 volumes*)

Imaginomicon:
Approaching Gateways to Higher Universes

Way of the Wizard: *Utilitarian Systemology*

Systemology-180: *Fast-Track to Ascension*

Systemology Backtrack:
Reclaiming Spiritual Power & Past-Life Memory

PUBLISHED BY THE **JOSHUA FREE** IMPRINT REPRESENTING

The Mardukite Academy of Systemology

mardukite.com